THE AMAZING JOURNEY OF CUPPA

His Quest to Find the Five Secrets of the Confident Mindset

MISSION 3

POSITIVITY

An exciting learning adventure teaching tweenagers (9-13 year olds) the Confident Mindset - self-belief, self-esteem, persistence, positivity, empathy and emotional resilience. Packed with positive messages, tests and activities!

On Behalf of Dad and Danni

Ross McWilliam

First published 2017 by Ross McWilliam Associates

ISBN 978-0-9956759-5-7

CONTENTS

MISSION THREE: POSITIVITY

No sooner had Cuppa waved goodbye to Ursula at Sheremetyevo International Airport, than he was flying out of Moscow on a big, white aeroplane with red tips in the shape of maple leaves on the wings. Looking out of the window at the snow on the ground he started to feel tired as all his recent exciting activities began to catch up with him. Before long, he had fallen into a deep sleep.

Some hours later Cuppa woke to the sound of the air stewardess offering him an in-flight snack.

"Well, hello there, young man. Would you like some juice and a few cookies?" said the air stewardess.

He was hungry, but also startled. The air stewardess looked familiar. Her dark hair was tied in a bun. Four buns, in fact; almost as if she had just walked out of a pop video. Her heavy eyebrows pointed down at her nose and her mouth was a thin red line. Cuppa looked up to read her name badge: Ms Rocky-Mountain-Fortress! He knew he had seen her before, but where?

Then Cuppa started to wonder about Pete Positivity. He didn't know where Pete lived, but was excited at the prospect of finding out!

The plane soon started its descent and over the tannoy system he heard the captain say, "Please fasten your seat belts. After our ten-hour flight, we are ten minutes away from landing at Lester B. Pearson International Airport in Toronto, Canada!"

Cuppa had never been to Canada, but he had heard many wonderful things about it: the Mounties, the bears, the Great Lakes, ice hockey, maple syrup, and the fabulous Rocky Mountains.

Before long, the plane had landed on the icy tarmac and all the passengers rushed off to the airport. Cuppa passed through passport control and waited for his suitcase at the revolving luggage carousel.

He felt nervous about meeting Pete Positivity, especially when he was on his own. Watching the metal carousel go round and round, he started to get dizzy and grabbed his dog tag. There was no Alf. Where was Alf when he needed him?

Then Cuppa remembered. Alf had helped him before when he arrived at Moscow Confidence First School. But he was so nervous. Couldn't Alf bend the rules and help him again?

There was still no sign of Alf, so Cuppa simply decided to relax, stick it out and wait. Within just a few minutes he heard a loud voice.

"Howdy, Cuppa!"

"Alf, is that you?" asked Cuppa.

"No, it's Pete!" said a big guy dressed in a checked shirt, blue faded jeans, huge tan boots and a massive cowboy hat. "Pete Positivity at your service! Grab your bags, buddy we are off to the CN Tower in Toronto to meet the First Nations Chief. He's the leader of the Canadian tribes and a direct descendant from the first peoples who roamed the plains of Canada."

"Howdy, Pete!" said Cuppa. "I can't wait to start our adventure!"

In no time at all, Cuppa and Pete Positivity were looking at the awesome CN Tower, built in 1976 and which was, at that time, the highest free-standing building in the world, at over 1,800 feet (548 metres).

The First Nations chief was on the top floor. He was dressed in an impressive coloured headset and flowing robe.

"Nice to see you, Pete. Who is your friend?" he asked, looking at Cuppa.

"Howdy, Chief Running Cloud. This is Chris Cupsworth and he has come all the way from the UK, via Russia, to learn about being positive."

"Hello, Chief Running Cloud," said Cuppa, thinking that he really did look unique! Before the chief could reply, Cuppa added, "But my friends call me Cuppa!"

"Very pleased to meet you, Cuppa. So you are here to learn about the positive mindset at Toronto Confidence First School?" asked the chief. Before Cuppa could answer, the chief carried on. "Today heralds the start of the First Nations Cultural Week. Look out over Toronto, Cuppa. You will see a vast concrete jungle. But beyond that, at the furthest northern point, you will see a mountain. That's where our school is, where we're hosting all the cultural activities. Your journey of positivity will start there!"

Cuppa started to wonder what he had got himself into. There would be many challenges and unique situations he would have to face and he would certainly need all his positivity just to survive!

The chief, Pete, and Cuppa took the elevator down the CN Tower and headed off to the mountain in the chief's big red four-by-four mountain ranger truck.

Within an hour, Cuppa could see the school. There were no concrete buildings or flags, as there had been at the other schools, just a clearing in a massive forest. Around seventy tent-like structures stood on the snow, together with several barking dogs, a corral of horses, a few open fires and hundreds of people wandering around. A big tree stood behind a stage. On closer inspection, Cuppa noticed some writing on the tree. "Toronto Confidence First School" had been etched on to it with natural resin, with a CUPPA logo.

Cuppa heard people chanting and noticed the smells of food cooking and wood burning. He had never known anything like it.

"Cuppa, your first lesson is in the school tepee over there," said Pete.

"A tepee....is that" said Cuppa. Before Cuppa said anything more which might get him into trouble, Pete interrupted him.

"You might know it as a tent, but a tepee is a spiritual home for us. It's also much bigger than the tents you're used to," said Pete.

As Cuppa stepped into the school tepee it was like walking inside Dr Who's Tardis: small on the outside, but massive inside. Around sixty children sat on the floor around a tree, listening to the teacher.

"Welcome to our tepee school, Cuppa. We've been expecting you," said the teacher.

"How do you know my name?" asked Cuppa.

"We know all about you, Cuppa, from our chief's air-stewardess connections," she said, winking at the rest of the class as if they had a big secret. "And you know nothing about us ... yet! So let's start with my name. It's Miss Brightside" said the small woman with the happy sort of face.

Cuppa thought that couldn't be her real name, but maybe it was some sort of First Nation name given to you to reflect your personality? It certainly seemed to suit her.

"Now, if I told you everyone's name," said Miss Brightside, "you would never remember them all, so that can wait for now while we start our positive learning journey together. First, we are going to play a word association game, to prepare you for the cultural games which start tomorrow at sunrise."

The other children grinned at each other, and a girl at the front of the class raised her arm. "Can I go first, miss?"

"Of course, Penny Mae. But remember, you must say the first word that comes into your head after I say my word. OK? Let's have a trial run," said Miss Brightside. "Royal."

Penny Mae responded. "Blue!"

"Ice."

"Hockey!"

"Pepsi."

"Max!"

"Well done, Penny Mae. You're a very confident person. Now let's play the game for real. Cuppa, are you ready?"

He did not feel ready at all, but he nodded anyway.

"I might say more than one word!" said Miss Brightside. This made Cuppa even more nervous.

"Ready? Let's start ... Nervous."

"Scared!"

"Terrified."

"Can't move."

"Problem."

"Disaster."

"Loser."

"Me!"

There was an awkward silence before Miss Brightside spoke. "Cuppa, do you realise you answered each of my words with a negative word?" asked Miss Brightside.

"No, miss," said Cuppa.

"You're bad at this game!"

"I guess I am," answered Cuppa.

"See, Cuppa, you've done it again. When you feel nervous you start to think negatively. You need to learn how to **turn a negative into a positive**. The first step towards changing your habits is to be aware of how your feelings are affecting you. Let Jenny Mae show you. OK, Jenny Mae, here we go! Rain."

"Sunshine!"

"Whoopee, Jenny Mae! Well done. You sisters are a real act - like my favourite movie!" Miss Brightside looked at Cuppa, "Do you want another go now?"

Cuppa nodded and awaited the first word.

"Nervous."

Cuppa thought about his feelings first, and then found an answer.

"Confident."

"Well done, Cuppa. Let's carry on. Terrified."

"Chilled, and ready for your next word, miss."

"I'm better than you," said Miss Brightside.

"In your dreams, miss," said Cuppa, smiling.

"Not good enough!"

"I'm unique!"

"Problem."

"Solution!"

"Wow, Cuppa! What a difference thinking about how you feel makes!"

The whole class cheered.

"Word associations are a great way to develop a positive attitude, Cuppa," said Miss Brightside. "But we need to take this attitude into real-life situations as well. We call this the **think-feel-do triangle**."

Cuppa had one of his '**Breakthrough Thoughts**' ...

Something as simple as thinking can help you feel better and become better ... wow!

"A great real-life example of this can be seen in the skills of Mia Hamm," said Miss Brightside. "She is the most famous female football player in the world. She was always talking about turning a negative into a positive in all the situations she faced in her matches. In fact, she's American and they call football – soccer! She plays in the USA, but often visits us here in Canada, especially during Cultural Week!" added Miss Brightside as she finally got Cuppa's full attention.

VIDEO – MIA HAMM

https://goo.gl/FBs9U5

A loud sound interrupted the lesson, like a big gong going off over and over again. Cuppa felt worried, but he could see from the faces of his classmates, as they jumped to their feet, that whatever was about to happen was something they were looking forward to.

"In fact, Cuppa," said Miss Brightside, "you're going to get an opportunity to demonstrate the action part of the triangle right now. That gong signals the start of the First Nations Cultural Week and we always begin with the Husky Dog Sled Race. This way, children."

As Cuppa followed her towards the centre of the camp he could hear several dogs barking. In the centre, he saw around twenty of them pulling on four sleds. Their breath was clear to see in the icy air, almost as if they were letting off steam.

A large, noisy crowd had gathered and Chief Running Cloud appeared on a stage at the front. Instantly, the whole place became silent to listen to him.

"Today, this hour, this very minute, our annual First Nations Cultural Week begins. There will be a number of activities to remember and celebrate the heritage of our people, starting now with the Husky Dog Sled Race."

"Hey, Cuppa, just look at those four sleds," said Pete. "I can see the Hank and Chuck Mack Twins in one, Jenny and Penny Mae in another, and Limping Elk and Hopping Elk in another."

"So who's riding in the fourth sled, Pete?" asked Cuppa.

"That must be us, partner!" said Pete.

"Attention, all riders! Please make sure you are ready to start," said the chief.

Pete jumped into the driver's seat while Cuppa reluctantly approached the passenger seat and sat down next to him. They lined up at the start with all the other sleds.

"The winner of the race is the team that wins both laps of the forest. After one lap, each sled must stop and change drivers," said the chief.

"Well, look at that. Old saucer boy in a sled," said Hank Mack, looking towards Cuppa.

"Ha, ha! He'll never do one lap, never mind win the race!" said Chuck.

Cuppa felt his anxiety levels rise. Pete quickly reassured him.

"Listen, Cuppa. They are only jealous that you are riding with the great Pete Positivity. Just remember to do as I say on the first lap and don't worry about them."

The gong sounded for the race to start. The Mack Twins stormed into an early lead. Pete managed to squeeze ahead of Jenny and Penny Mae, and the Elks.

As the forest approached, the Mack Twins were pushing their husky dogs hard. The blades on their sled cut up the ice with a rasping sound, sending ice particles all over Pete and Cuppa. Soon they were out of sight behind the treeline and all that could be heard were the dogs barking as they pulled harder and harder.

Cuppa noticed a look on Pete's face. He was losing, but he wasn't nervous. He actually seemed to be smiling.

"Hey, Pete, why are you smiling? We are second, not first!" said Cuppa.

"Don't worry, just focus and think-feel-do." said Pete, holding the reins tightly.

He repeated the words, this time shouting them. "THINK-FEEL-DO! THINK-FEEL-DO!"

The first lap was almost over when Cuppa noticed that the Mack Twins were slowing down. Sure enough their dogs had tired, and Pete was using his experience to steer their sled through all the fast ice to gain extra speed. As both sleds approached the finishing line, Pete was closing in with every step of their dogs. The Mack Twins were looking over their shoulders.

As the final bend approached, Pete said, "Lean out, Cuppa ... now!"

Like magic, their sled hit a bump and flew through the air past the Mack Twins and over the finishing line. Pete and Cuppa had won the first lap!

Pete changed seats so Cuppa could drive. Cuppa was so terrified his teeth were chattering, but Pete just smiled and clapped him on the shoulder.

"Chill out, my friend, and don't listen to **the Chimp**."

"Who on earth is the chimp?"

"The chimp is a powerful part of your brain that's always telling you that you can't do it, that somebody else is better. It makes you believe these negative thoughts and then you start acting like you've already lost. The secret is to recognise it's the Chimp talking and replace it by **doing a Jessica**!" said Pete.

"Doing a who?"

"Imagine a young, strong minded three year old girl who says all positive words to make herself feel good. She stands in front of the mirror and says stuff like, 'I can do it! I'm great! I can't lose!' She stops the chimp dead in its tracks!"

"But what happens if you ignore the Chimp and do a Jessica, and things still go badly?" asked Cuppa.

"Well, use the opportunity to do more practice and preparation. You can even ask your friends, parents, teachers about ways you can improve!" said Pete.

Cuppa took on board Pete's words of advice. However, it was now time to start the second race and there was no time to practise. The gong went and everyone raced off.

Cuppa held on to the reins tightly and hoped the dogs would just keep pulling. As the trees flashed by he quickly became dizzy.

"Alf, where the heck are you?" he screamed.

Pete looked at Cuppa. "Who's Alf?"

"Er, nobody!" said Cuppa, thinking Alf had deserted him again.

Behind them the Mack Twins were catching up. Jenny and Penny Mae had dropped behind the Elks.

As the next bend approached Cuppa lost control of the reins, the dogs turned round and seemed to smile at him before slipping. Their sled spun round and round and a hazy, icy mist surrounded them. In that split second both the Mack Twins and the Elks overtook them. Cuppa felt Willie Fail had something to do with it. He grabbed the dog tag.

"Howdy, Cuppa. I thought I'd see if you could do it on your own. But I guess you need a little help to rein things in – stop you going to the dogs!" laughed Alf. "So, let me help you take a weight off your mind. Here are your choices ..."

Choice One: you continue to stay nervous and just hope you don't hurt yourself.

Choice Two: you stop letting the Chimp affect you, do a Jessica and give it 100 per cent.

Choice Three: you stop letting the Chimp affect you, do a Jessica, but hold back.

WHICH CHOICE WOULD YOU MAKE?

Let's look into the future and see what happens as a result of your choices:

Choice One: the rest of the race is a nightmare; you are just trying to avoid injury. You lose but you are happy you didn't get hurt. Some of the First Nations people think you chickened out and some thought you did OK. You now feel a bit sad you didn't give it a better shot and you wonder what else you might chicken out of during the Cultural Week.

Choice Two: you recognise the Chimp is trying to put you down. As soon as you realise that, you do a Jessica and give yourself a great chance of winning and not getting hurt! Everybody sees you being positive and your friends enjoy being with you.

Choice Three: you recognise the Chimp is trying to put you down and Jessica is helping you ... but you don't fully believe it because you know the other drivers have more experience. Do you let a great chance slip through your hands?

Cuppa picked choice two and decided to give it 100 per cent. He recognised the nasty work of the Chimp and listened to Jessica for once! He was putting the odds in his favour for a successful outcome.

With increased belief, he chased after the Mack Twins and the Elks. He was closing in on the Mack Twins. As the twins rounded another corner, Hank threw a snowball at Hopping Elk, who was driving. For a split second Hopping Elk took his eyes off the course and his sled hit a hidden rock and overturned!

The Mack Twins were pulling away and had only one bend left to negotiate to win the second lap. In a split second Cuppa made a decision and stopped his sled.

He ran across to the Elks and helped them to their feet. Hopping and Limping Elk were bruised and a little shocked, but otherwise they were fine.

"Hey, thanks, Cuppa, but we may have lost you the race," said Hopping Elk.

"That's OK. Winning isn't everything," said Cuppa.

The Elks, Pete and Cuppa carried on to the finish line where the Mack Twins had arrived first this time, ahead of Jenny and Penny Mae. The whole race was a tie between the Mack Twins and Pete and Cuppa. Chief Running Cloud had to make a final decision.

"After two laps we have a tie. But in First Nations heritage we must have a winner. According to our tradition, I will ask the losers to decide."

Hopping and Limping didn't say anything. They just pointed to Pete and Cuppa. The whole crowd went wild. They clapped and shouted their approval.

Out of the corner of his eye Cuppa could see Chuck Mack clapping!

That evening the First Nation elders held a celebration dinner dance. It was very informal and nobody wore ballgowns or black ties, but it was still very special. Various tribes took it in turns to sing their native songs while some of the women danced to the music. Cuppa hadn't seen anything quite like it, except on TV - and this was so much better. He was relaxed and thoroughly enjoying the entertainment when ... something happened!

Hopping and Limping Elk, having recovered from their crash, had decided to sing and dance for the tribes. The music was a solo drum beat to which Hopping Elk and Limping Elk did a sort of ritual dance. Cuppa wondered if this was how they had got their names.

Chief Running Cloud motioned Cuppa over to the top table where all the elder tribespeople were sitting.

"Hey, Cuppa. Given that you are on your positivity journey and you seem to be enjoying the dance, how about you demonstrate your positivity by joining in with the Elks?"

Cuppa wanted to say yes, but something inside stopped him. He had danced in Russia at the casual T-shirt dancing competition, but this kind of dancing was very different from anything he was used to. And he knew he was no good at singing! In his mind he thought about the think-feel-do triangle, but he still couldn't do it. He then thought about the Chimp, and Jessica. But still he felt frozen with fear.

"All right, Cuppa," said the chief. "You've come a long way today, further than many others. But I suspect you may need some more practice with what Pete and Miss Brightside have been teaching you. That's OK for today, but remember sometimes in life we have to just do it. Maybe soon, on your journey, you'll accept that challenge and **step outside your comfort zone**."

Cuppa was immediately relieved. He relaxed and watched the evening's entertainment. However, a small part of him wished he'd just got up, sung a song and danced. His opportunity had gone now, but maybe there would be another one in the future.

The morning soon rolled around and there was an air of anticipation. Everyone had gathered in the clearing and waited for Chief Running Cloud to speak.

"In years gone by, our tribespeople would travel around the Great Lakes of Canada and America in search of fish in the lakes, animals in the woods and birds in the trees. Now we must follow in our ancient ancestors' footsteps. But rather than search for food, we travel around the Great Lakes and collect donations for charity.

"Our charity this year is the Rick Hansen Foundation which helps support people who are disabled and mainly use wheelchairs. Our lodge has been nominated to cover Lake Ontario, a journey of 527 miles or 848 kilometres. We are going to nominate Miss Brightside to lead it. This year the nominated people will cover the journey over five days - riding bicycles!" said Chief Running Cloud, rubbing his big hands together.

This was an incredible distance to cycle. Cuppa had only ever cycled to the shops and back and that scared feeling was returning faster and faster with every breath.

"Since we witnessed some sporting rivalry in the Husky Dog Sled Race, we, the elders, have decided to promote sportsmanship. Rather than this being an outright race, all the competitors who raced against each other yesterday will be on the same team for the next five days. This should help you all work together in the spirit of the First Nations."

The next few hours were all about preparation for the charity event. Miss Brightside collected the bikes and asked the Mack Twins to check each was working properly and had a repair kit. Hopping and Limping Elk were in charge of food and water supplies, while Jenny and Penny Mae were to plot the course on the map, including where to pitch their mini tepees at night. Cuppa and Pete were in charge of collecting donations. They found some buckets to collect the money, and made signs which would fit on each of their bikes. Another pupil, Quiet Ethan, or Et as he liked to be known, was in charge of all technology because he had a flair for anything that beeped.

By lunchtime the group was ready. They all knew that this was a big challenge, but they relished the chance to prove themselves worthy of their First Nations tribespeople. Cuppa wanted to prove himself too, but his nerves and doubts were getting the better of him again.

The group set off at a fast pace with the adrenalin pumping round almost everyone.

"Slow down, girls!" called Miss Brightside, as Jenny and Penny Mae cycled out of sight with the Mack Twins in hot pursuit. She sighed. "Pete, you go ahead and check on them. I'll stay with the others."

She brought her bicycle alongside Cuppa's. "You look tired, Cuppa. I bet you're thinking that you'll never make the distance?"

Cuppa nodded, too tired even to talk.

"Remember yesterday in class, when you turned a negative into a positive?"

Cuppa nodded again.

"Well, today I want to share the story of how Rick Hansen turned a major negative into a positive. He's Canadian, which is a great start! But he became paralysed as a teenager and had to use a wheelchair for the rest of his life. Rather than letting this get him down, he saw it as an opportunity to change things for the better, for others! He campaigned for greater awareness for disabled people."

"How did he do that, Miss Brightside?"

"He went all round the world in his wheelchair and it took him two years, two months and two days to complete his journey. While he travelled he collected money for his charity, the Rick Hansen Foundation, and today the charity has raised millions of dollars for disabled people in Canada, and throughout the world. He always said that if you can think it, you can achieve it. I want you to practise this, Cuppa - I call it the **TA Principle**!" said Miss Brightside.

VIDEO - RICK HANSEN

https://goo.gl/oYikcD

Cuppa smiled and thought about his tiredness. "I get it, miss. Ta for the story!"

"And another thing, Cuppa. He said that his best years were still ahead of him. He always looked on the bright side. And right now our designated campsite is ahead of us, and you will be able to have a rest."

The sun was starting to go down, and Pete and the breakaway group were sitting down at the campsite which Jenny and Penny had found with their navigation skills.

Everyone pitched in putting up the mini tepee. It was a simple brown colour on the outside, but on the inside wild animals were painted in bright colours. Hanging down from the middle was a dangling collection of strange shapes made out of feathers, arrowheads and beads. This was a First Nation dreamcatcher, which caught bad dreams like flies in a spider's web, and let good ones through. After their evening meal, Hank and Chuck decided to share a story with the others.

"D'you know, a few years ago, at this very spot on the shores of Lake Ontario, an elder from our tribe was eaten alive!" said Hank, looking across at Chuck.

"Yep, and it was no other than Little Crawling Cup," said Chuck, winking at Hank.

"In fact, a brown bear was hiding in the woods and as Little Crawling Cup sat in his tepee, the bear pounced on him. Little Crawling Cup wasn't a fast runner and the bear caught him and pulled him limb from limb!"

Cuppa could feel the blood draining from his face. He wasn't sure whether they were winding him up or telling a true story. Either way, he wasn't looking forward to sleeping in the great Canadian wilderness.

But, like everyone else, Cuppa soon fell asleep. Tired from his physical exertions, but more tired from worrying about finishing the charity cycle ... and the thought of a bear eating him alive!

The next day was soon upon them and the sun rose in the clear blue sky. It was still cold, but the dry roads made for good cycling conditions.

"This morning," said Miss Brightside, "I'll divide you in to two groups and I'll cycle between you. Cuppa and Pete, you can cycle with Hopping and Limping Elk."

Cuppa was pleased about that. The Elks were real team players, always trying their best but never at the expense of anyone else. However, he was to discover that they had not always been like that!

"Cuppa, can I tell you a story about how we got our names?" said Limping Elk.

"Yes, as long as it isn't scary!" said Cuppa.

"Well, when we were much younger we had a reputation for being a little cruel, a bit like Hank and Chuck, I suppose. We didn't hurt anyone, but we played loads of tricks on children and adults alike. The elders thought we needed to be taught a lesson. So every time we played a cruel trick, the elders would make us go into the wild and sleep on our own for a night. At first we were a bit scared, but we soon started to enjoy it. It didn't feel like a punishment, more like a reward for being bad. This infuriated the elders. Then, one night, we decided to see if we could catch an elk and prove to the elders that we were real men. We took a rope from the camp and went in search. We saw a small baby elk by a river and thought we would lasso it. As we approached, Hopping slipped and fell in the river. The little elk started to panic and charged at Hopping and caught his foot with its horns. I turned to run away, but the elk caught up with me and bashed into my leg.

"When we returned to camp we were badly shaken but unhurt, except that we were limping and hopping. The whole camp wondered what had happened. When we told them our story they all started to laugh. Chief Running Cloud then gave us our names.

"But that was only the start really. We realised what it felt like to be laughed at, and we decided to stop playing cruel tricks on people and try to be helpful instead. The more helpful we were, the more people liked us and it became a **good habit**!"

Cuppa's journey of positivity was really coming together and the next couple of days just flew by. But as much as he was enjoying his journey, he was missing his mum and dad, especially at night. One evening, Miss Brightside found him sitting alone in the tepee.

"Cuppa," she said, "I think you may be suffering from the dreaded disease which the First Nations call alonenauseous. Or, in plain English, you're homesick! Am I right?"

Cuppa nodded.

"Don't worry, I know a cure. I'll send Quiet Ethan to you with his laptop."

Presently, Quiet Ethan arrived and sat down beside Cuppa without a word. As he logged on to his laptop, a message popped up. It was an automated voice message, the type that talks to you.

"Et Skype home," said the message.

Once the Skype system was activated, Cuppa connected to his mum and dad over 3,000 miles (4,800km) away in the UK.

"Mum, Dad ... it's me ... I've missed you!" said Cuppa, trying to hold back his tears.

"Hey, Chris, great to hear and see you! Are you having a fun time?" asked his mum.

"Yes, Mum, it's brilliant! I just wanted to see you ... and Dad, of course," said Cuppa.

"We all miss you, Chris," said his dad.

"Dad, what's that music I can hear in the background. Is it from Annie?" asked Cuppa.

"There's no music on. We were just playing cards when you called," said his mum.

"Wow, that's strange. I could have sworn I heard that Annie music that Danni liked!" said Cuppa.

"You must be tired, so why don't you get some rest and we'll see you very soon," said his mum, before adding, "Don't go listening to that chimp!"

Cuppa wondered briefly how she knew about the positivity stuff. Maybe she had been reading up on it. Never mind, he thought, I'm just glad I got a chance to see and hear my folks back home.

He said his goodbyes and logged off feeling so much better, thanks to Quiet Ethan and his skill with the laptop.

By the end of the fourth day they had covered 500 miles and the end was in sight. The final part of the journey was all downhill and

Cuppa was looking forward to freewheeling down to where the camp would be that night.

Just as Cuppa started his descent, Hank Mack rode past giggling to himself. This was strange behaviour, even for him, and Cuppa wondered what he was up to. He didn't have to wait long to find out.

Faster and faster went Cuppa down the hill. He was loving every single second, feeling the warm air rush past his face. A small bend approached.

Hank Mack cycled next to him and shouted out, "Hey, Bradley Cupcake Wiggins! Have you tried your brakes recently?"

Cuppa tried his brakes and they didn't work. His mood turned instantly from happy-go-lucky to intensely fearful. What was he going to do?

His first reaction was to panic, and then to be angry with Hank Mack, who had obviously known that the brakes would fail, and had perhaps even damaged them on purpose. But in a split second Cuppa remembered to think-feel-do. How could he change a negative into a positive? His next thought was one of real clarity.

As the bend approached, he knew he had to slow down or he would fall off the bike into the valley below. He steered towards Chuck Mack.

"Chuck, help me! I'm going to stay on my bike, but grab your bike seat. Put your brakes on as hard as you can when I shout 'Now!'" cried Cuppa.

Cuppa's bike was going faster than Chuck's and he had only one chance to grab hold.

As Cuppa approached Chuck he yelled out, "Now brake, Chuck!"

Chuck applied the brakes with such pressure that little ribbons of black smoke appeared from beneath his tyres. Chuck squeezed tighter and more smoke billowed out from both tyres as they threatened to catch fire.

The metal in the wheel started to touch the tarmac of the road. The screeching, grinding noise of metal on tarmac was horrendous, but it slowed Cuppa down.

Within a few more seconds both bikes had come to a stop, inches from the bend. Chuck had saved the day. Cuppa looked round for Hank, and saw him slinking away into the trees.

It was the final night of camping and although Cuppa was tired he kept waking up. He began to watch the swirling dreamcatcher in the middle of the tepee. Round and round it went as the wind whistled outside and the trees creaked in the breeze. Then he heard another noise. Was it that Willie Fail again? Or was it a bear, the same bear that the Mack Twins had mentioned on the first night? Cuppa reached for his dog tag.

"Hey, Cuppa. It's Alf the Bear here. I barely recognised you in all your fancy Lycra. Now let's paws for some choices," said Alf, laughing to himself.

"Alf, I thought you were the bear coming to eat me alive!" said Cuppa, so relieved to see Alf that he was almost happy to hear his jokes.

"No, no, no, Cuppa. I'm strictly vegetarian! I am here to give you some choices because you seem to need some guidance on your positivity journey. But these choices are a little different because they are all based around the **today result and tomorrow promise**. Before you interrupt me, let me explain, dear Little Crawling Cup. I can see you are worrying too much sometimes, so I want to share something with you which I am sure will help.

"Write down three things that turned out positive today, and then decide on at least one good positive thing you are going to do tomorrow. It may even be something outside your comfort zone. You then promise yourself, friends, teachers or your parents, that you will try to make it come true. And remember that the chimp is at its strongest at night, so doing this at the end of the day will really protect you! So, here are your choices ..."

Choice One: you keep worrying about everything bad that might happen to you.

Choice Two: you focus on your today result and tomorrow promise and make it a habit, even when things don't quite work out the way you wanted.

Choice Three: you focus on your today result and tomorrow promise, but get downhearted when things don't work out.

WHICH CHOICE WOULD YOU MAKE?

Let's look into the future and see what happens as a result of your choices:

Choice One: your worrying gets out of control and you start to be afraid of everything. You soon become the weakest link in the cycling team and spoil the trip for yourself and others. Worst of all, this bad habit of negative self-belief persists after the trip.

Choice Two: you write down three positive things for today. One: you have made some good friends on the bike ride. Two: you have cycled 500 miles. Three: you are raising money for charity. Your tomorrow promise is to step outside your comfort zone. You keep to your word and everything turns out great tomorrow when you have the opportunity to impress a famous person.

Choice Three: you write down three positive things for today. One: you have made some good friends on the bike ride. Two: you have cycled 500 miles. Three: you are raising money for charity. Your tomorrow promise is to step outside your comfort zone. You miss an opportunity to do this when you get nervous and then you miss more opportunities throughout your journey.

Cuppa picked choice two because he was getting tired of worrying and wanted to push himself. He knew he had the support of others.

Cuppa had one of his '**Breakthrough Thoughts**' ...

The comfort zone is where I want to be ... but not all the time!

The next day started early with the birds chirping in the trees. It was almost as if they were showing their respect for the tremendous charity bike ride. The final few miles were soon cycled and the group of young people proudly returned to the First Nations camp, where final preparations were being made for the official closure of the First Nations Cultural Week. Many VIP guests had been invited, including the main guest Chief Frozen 'Let it Flow' who had earned his name by being the one chief who could break up the river ice in early spring. Other guests included Chief Roaming Bi and son, Chief Runny Maple Syrup, Chief Many Fast Rivers and his wife Flo, Chief Tain Tank and Chief Slow Walker, who always seemed to turn up last!

Chief Running Cloud made a closing speech.

"What a week we have witnessed. Many people have overcome their own fears to help others. We have celebrated the heritage of our forefathers and, in the long tradition of the First Nations, we have welcomed people into our way of life. One of these people is Chris Cuspworth. Now, before we eat our final meal together, I would like to ask Cuppa, as he is affectionately called, to say thanks to the animals, birds, plants, water and the land."

"Wow, that is going to take me all day" said Cuppa, looking at Pete.

"No worries, Cuppa. It's just a short speech that's said before eating. It's only in front of over two hundred people!" said Pete.

His words filled Cuppa with absolute fear. How could he address a crowd of over two hundred people, especially when he'd never done that before?

A smiling woman came over to them. "Really, Pete, you mustn't scare Cuppa. Let me work with him and practise saying his thank you speech. Just give me a few minutes and we will give you a positive result!" said the VIP guest. It was none other than Mia Hamm, the famous American soccer player.

Pete stalled Chief Running Cloud by telling the crowd that he wanted to thank the Canadian people for helping to raise $2,500 for the Rick Hansen Fund. While the crowd cheered, Mia helped Cuppa.

"I'm not sure I can do this, Mia. People will be watching me, won't they?"

"Yes, they will, but it'll be a great opportunity to show everyone just how much progress you've made. An opportunity to show them how positive and unique you are and how you can take on challenges. Here's a tip that might help you, it's called **afformation**. I want you to think of a reason why you are going to make a great speech. Find evidence from your past successes to remind you of your abilities."

"Well, since arriving in Canada, I have said yes to almost every opportunity, like dog sledding and cycle riding. But I also turned down an opportunity to dance with Hopping and Limping Elk. I don't want to miss another opportunity and I did promise myself that I would get outside my comfort zone today. I have shown some courage and now this courage is going to get me through this speech!"

VIDEO - CARA THE COMPLETER

https://goo.gl/FduhDw

"If you need any more reasons to make this speech, just take a look across at the horse corral," said Mia.

As Cuppa looked across he could see a number of horses, and a few tribespeople standing around the middle where one horse was on its own. But it wasn't really on its own. The sight that met Cuppa's eyes was so surprising he had to strain his eyes to believe what he was seeing.

Sitting on the horse was none other than Quiet Ethan.

"Chief Running Cloud told me that Quiet Ethan has been impressed by the way you handled yourself in the Husky Dog Sled Race and the charity bike ride. You never gave in to failure and always tried to remain positive. Ethan was inspired by you, so he asked to see if he could sit on a horse for the very first time!" said Mia. "Now, are you going to let everyone down and not say a few special words?"

Chief Running Cloud banged the dinner gong and it was time for Cuppa to speak.

He cleared his throat.

"Please bow your heads.

Thank you for this food,

Keep us in a pleasant mood.

Bless the chef and all who serve us.

From indigestion, Chief Running Cloud preserve us!

With all these plates, and all these cups,

Thank goodness I'm not doing the washing up!"

Everyone seemed slightly shocked into silence.

"Enjoy!" said Cuppa, remembering what the staff at their favourite restaurant used to say to him and Danni. Everyone laughed. They seemed to finally like his sense of humour!

"Well done, Cuppa. That was awesome. Were you nervous?" asked Mia.

"Not a nerve in sight!" he said triumphantly. It wasn't true, of course, and he was still shaking, but he had done it, and now he felt on top of the world!

"Cuppa, are you ready for your next mission?" asked Chief Running Cloud.

"Yep, bring it on. Where to next?" said Cuppa.

"You are off to meet Paula Perception and she lives in ..."

MISSION 3 VIDEOS

https://goo.gl/RSr4fJ

KEYWORDS

Turn a Negative into a Positive - make a negative situation better by seeing it as positive.

Think-Feel-Do Triangle - if you think negatively, you can start to feel negative and then you might act negatively. Turn this around by thinking, feeling and acting positively.

The Chimp - the negative part of our brain that wants us to fail.

Doing a Jessica - creating a really positive mood by saying good things to yourself.

Step Outside Your Comfort Zone - doing something that is new to you or scares you, but after you've done it you will have made progress.

TA Principle - think you can do it and you can achieve it.

Good Habit - showing good behaviours without even thinking about it.

Today Result and Tomorrow Promise - the today result is to write down all the good things you did today, and the tomorrow promise is to write down all the good things you will do tomorrow.

Afformation - Use evidence of past successes to believe you will be successful when a challenge presents itself.

THINK AND CHECK!

Reflect on what you have read in the story so far to make sure you understand

- **What did Cuppa learn when he played the word association game? How did this help him?**
- **How did Cuppa win the husky dog sled race?**
- **When Cuppa realised that his brakes weren't working, how did he stop himself from panicking?**
- **Cuppa learnt that it was good to step outside his comfort zone and try new things from time to time. How did he feel after not dancing with the Elks? How was this different from when he made a speech in front of 200 people?**

Now you can complete Mission 3 activities!

"I like watching animals play. I'm not so sure about racing them if they don't want to race. But when they do love to race, I love watching them. Especially if they are horses, and especially if they are running around Cartmel Race Track!"

Danni

MISSION THREE: ACTIVITIES

1.

Positive You? (eight points - one per answer)

Find a friend and try this to challenge your negative thoughts. Fill in the empty boxes with a positive response to the negative comment.

Negative Thoughts	Positive Thoughts
1. I am too busy to do my homework.	I am never too busy for developing me – I make time!
2. I am too tired to do my homework.	
3. I don't like problems.	
4. I am not like the others in some ways.	
5. I don't have many friends.	
6. I keep failing.	
7. I am not good enough.	
8. I always have negative thoughts.	
Two points each if you can make up your own negative and positive sayings (eight points)	

9	
10	
11	
12	

WHAT ABOUT THIS IDEA?

Can you add some more negative thoughts and positive responses?

The key is to try to own that statement and use it regularly so that it becomes a good habit.

LET'S TALK

In pairs, or a larger group, discuss:

1. How you feel when you say something negative.

2. How you feel when somebody reminds you to be more positive.

3. How you really feel when you say something positive, especially if at the time everything feels negative?

Even an adult can help - ask them about the Mission 3 **Trouble Shooter Toolkit Chart / Top Tips and Specific Barriers To Learning.**

2.

Match Game (ten points - one point per matching pair)

Draw twenty squares on a piece of card and then cut up the squares. From the activity above, write a positive thought or word on ten of the squares and then write a negative thought or word on the other ten.

Then place all the squares face down. The task now is to match up the negative thought or word with the positive thought or word. Two points per pair.

Fragile: agile

Sad: happy

Can't: can

It's a challenge of memory and patience, especially if you are awaiting a turn. A great task to reinforce learning!

3.

Compliments (ten points: two points per compliment)

Make up a positive sentence about five people you know.

It doesn't have to be long, just as long as you mean it. ONLY accept positive statements, e.g. Peter, I like the way you always hold the door open for others.

1.

2.

3.

4.

5.

WHAT ABOUT THIS IDEA?

Phrases could include:

Turn a negative into a positive.

Think-Feel-Do.

The Chimp.

Doing a Jessica.

The best years are ahead of me.

LET'S TALK

Do you worry...about exams, performing in public, making new friends, going to a new school?

Even an adult can help - ask them about the Mission 3 **Trouble Shooter Toolkit Chart / Top Tips and Specific Barriers To Learning.**

HOTSHOT

4.

Intensive Learning Lounge (ILL) Challenge (ten points: one point for each word described and one point for each word guessed)

Watch all, or some, of the videos below. From your chosen videos, pick out five key words.

MISSION 3 VIDEOS

https://goo.gl/RSr4fJ

Write them down below without your partner seeing them. It's top secret for now!

We are now ready to play guess my five words. Use your skills to describe each word to your partner, one at a time, without saying the actual word.

After you've read out your five words, it's your turn to guess your partner's words.

5.

Multiple Choice (twelve points: three points per answer)

Try these multiple choice questions. Be brave ... do it without any support!

1. The Chimp is something in your head that:

- [ ] A Must always be obeyed
- [ ] B Must be ignored
- [ ] C Must be listened to sometimes
- [ ] D All of the above

2. Doing a Jessica is:

- [ ] A Thinking negative things and letting these thoughts affect you
- [ ] B Saying negative things and letting these words affect you
- [ ] C Saying positive words that help you
- [ ] D None of the above

3. The TA principle is:

- [ ] A Thinking you will achieve success now
- [ ] B Thinking you will achieve success sometime
- [ ] C Thinking you will achieve success soon
- [ ] D All of the above

4. An Afformation is:

- ☐ **A** Thinking positive thoughts
- ☐ **B** Giving reasons why you will be successful
- ☐ **C** Hoping for success
- ☐ **D** Giving excuses to accept failure

6.

Reflection – Positive Vision Board Activity (twelve points: four points per box)

Create a vision board or a simple picture board of some of your experiences or achievements so far in your life. Rather than writing words only, draw pictures with a few key words.

Try to include two things you struggled with in the past and two things you are struggling with in the present, and then draw them in the future when you have beaten them.

PAST

Failed interview for cleaning cars.

Showed resilience and creativity and started my own car cleaning business.

PRESENT

Failed some School tests

Missed a penalty at football

FUTURE

Revised and learned the lessons from last time.

Practice and trained had and learnt lessons from last time.

Complete the vision board below.

PAST

PRESENT

FUTURE

WHAT ABOUT THIS IDEA?

Letting the Chimp win.

Not being positive with Jessica.

Not doing enough practice and preparation.

Not having enough experience.

Poor comments from others affecting you

Can you use teacher feedback and adult guidance?

LET'S TALK

Compare your vision board to somebody else's. What are the similarities and differences?

Even an adult can help - ask them about the Mission 3 **Trouble Shooter Toolkit Chart / Top Tips and Specific Barriers To Learning.**

HOTShot

Or

Create your Own Afformation Card (twelve points)

This is a chance to use an established saying, or create your own saying, on one side of a card, with reasons on the back about why you are going to be successful. Chris might create one called success-not-yet. He might draw images of what success looks like for him, but give reasons as to why he is going to achieve success, e.g. being prepared to practise, listening to other people's guidance and feedback, using the TA Principle and valuing his qualities and achievements.

Here are some examples!

FRONT

"EVERY DAY DO SOMETHING THAT WILL INCH YOU CLOSE TO A BETTER TOMORROW."

DON'T LIMIT YOUR CHALLENGES.

CHALLENGE YOUR LIMITS.

YOU CAN NEVER CROSS THE OCEAN UNLESS YOU HAVE THE COURAGE TO LOSE SIGHT OF THE SHORE.

STRENGTH

A RIVER CUTS THROUGH A ROCK NOT BECAUSE OF ITS POWER BUT ITS PERSISTENCE

BACK

I am going to be successful because...
....I have practised and taken advice about how to score penalties

WHAT ABOUT THIS IDEA?

Write down sayings that are positive, with reasons or evidence showing why you will be successful. Can you about what sayings you have heard and like. Be aware of poor examples of sayings that have flawed thinking, e.g. 'no pain, no gain' is not always correct!

7.

Positivity Poster Time (ten points)

Create a poster based on Mission Three.

Perhaps make a list first and then see if you can find evidence to support each point, e.g. qualities and achievements are more important than appearance; this is in evidence when you value people for their qualities rather than appearance.

8.

Cuppa's Top Tips (twenty points)

- ✓ Don't let yourself down by using ____________ words with others. Those words can be the start of a ______________ spiral where self-__________ is destroyed and ________________ is never achieved. Always try and be ____________.

- ✓ ____________ positive thinking regularly – it can soon turn into an automatic good habit where positive thoughts, words, feelings and actions occur naturally. Dismiss ______________ as soon as it enters your mind. Replace it with a ____________.

- ✓ When you think of reasons why you are going to be successful before you perform a task this is called an ________________.

- ✓ Tell your parents or friends at least __________ good things you did today. This is called the ___________________ and helps you become more confident.

- ✓ Tell your parents or friends at least ______ good thing you are going to do tomorrow. This is called the ___________________.

- ✓ Both the Today Result and Tomorrow Promise are great examples of a ____________________.

- ✓ Take ____________________ when they arrive. You may just enjoy the chance to show people what you can do!
- ✓ If you can ____________ it, you can ______________ it. This is the ______________________.
- ✓ When you talk, think and feel positive, you are in ________________________________.
- ✓ If you get nervous just __________________________.

WORD BANK

Positive / Esteem / Tomorrow Promise / Opportunities

Achieve / Downward / Positive Self Talk / Today Result

Negative / Practise / Think Feel Do / One / Think / Three

Afformation / Jessica / TA Principle / The Chimp

Confidence / Good Habit

WHAT ABOUT THIS IDEA?

What about a timed challenge?

Now colour in the Treemendous Total with your percentage success level: 20, 40, 60, 80 or 100!

Finally, always finish off with REAL FUN. Try This Game!

POSITIVE BINGO

Choice One

Use the words below to have a game of bingo. Choose a bingo caller and when you hear your word called, cross it out. When you have three in a row in any direction shout 'line bingo!' If it's a tie, ask each person to give a definition of each word.

Afformations	**Today Result**	**Comfort Zone**
Doing a Jessica	**Good Habits**	**TA Principle**
The Chimp	**Think-Feel-Do Triangle**	**Tomorrow Promise**

Choice Two

Make up your own words from all your learning. Now there's a challenge!

SO, WHAT HAVE WE LEARNT?

When we think negatively or act negatively towards others we can soon start a downward spiral which can result in losing self-esteem and confidence in yourself and others.

When we think positively, we can start to feel positive then act positive. This is called the think-feel-do triangle.

Don't let the negative chimp into your head. Replace it with a Jessica. This is a positive saying that helps us be successful.

An afformation is when we think of all the reasons why we are going to be successful before we have to perform a task. If we are not as successful as we want we may have to practice and prepare more, or even ask those we trust for advice.

Try to buy a diary and write down at least three good things you do each day - this is the today result. Write down at least one good thing you are going to do tomorrow - this is the tomorrow promise.

If you can think it you can achieve it - this is the TA Principle.

Above all, talk positively to yourself; become your best friend on your journey to success now or success-not-yet!

OPTIONAL CHALLENGE

Smarter Confidence (no marks: this brings intrinsic reward)

CUPPA wants to know whether you can complete this table.

Criteria	When did I do this? Score one (low) to five (high)
I worked in a challenging way and pushed my thinking.	
I had no fear of being judged.	
I was resilient and kept going when things got difficult (this could be distractions, past lessons, negative memories)	
I demonstrated no fear of failure.	
I kept practising, used effort and found flow.	
I accepted feedback and was patient.	
I worked as a team.	

SELF-REFLECTION EFFORT GRADE

CUPPA also wants to know how much effort you put into that challenge. Circle the box that describes your effort.

5 Total focus and in flow, wanting to achieve success and constantly searched for different ways to solve challenges, not distracted.

4 Mainly focused and mainly in flow, wanting to achieve success most of the time, and some searching for different ways to solve challenges, slight distraction.

3 Intermittent focus and stop-start flow, wanting success but not prepared to really stretch, and slowly got frustrated, some distraction.

2 Little focus and little flow. Let go of responsibility for effort, got really frustrated and tired out. Only did some work, distracted.

1 Not interested and no flow unless it's really easy. Watched the clock. Can't Be Bothered (CBB), totally distracted

Congratulations on completing your journey so far! Full steam ahead! Continue to Mission Four.

MISSION THREE – ANSWERS

1. Peer Positive List (maximum sixteen points: two per answer)

Here are some sample answers - there will be many others. The key is that it must make sense and "ring a bell" for you, i.e. you must try to own that statement and use it regularly so that it becomes a good habit.

Negative Thoughts	Positive Thoughts
I am too busy to do my homework.	I am never too busy for developing me - make time!
I am too tired to do my homework.	Don't make excuses - dig deep find that energy!
I don't like problems.	I love a challenge!
I am not like the others in some ways.	I am unique!
I don't have many friends.	Make some new friends!
I keep failing.	It's just success-not-yet as long as I practise and work hard!
I am not good enough.	I am worth it!
I always have negative thoughts.	Turn the negative into a positive with Jessica!

Eight points for creating four more negative and positive sayings!

2. Match Game (maximum ten points - one point per pair)

This can be played in pairs or small groups. It is a challenge of memory and patience, especially when awaiting a turn. A great task to reinforce learning!

3. Compliments (maximum ten points: two per answer)

Make up a positive sentence about five other people you know - it does not have to be long just as long as you mean it. Accept positive statements only.

4. ILL Activity (maximum ten points)

This is a describing game and guessing game. One point for describing a word and one point for guessing. A maximum of five words = ten points maximum.

5. Multiple Choice

(twelve points maximum: three points per answer)

1. The chimp is something in your head that:

A Must always be obeyed

B Must be ignored

C Must be listened to sometimes

D All of the above

2. Doing a Jessica is:

A Thinking negative things and letting these thoughts affect you

B Saying negative things and letting these thoughts affect you

C Saying positive words that help you

D None of the above

3. The TA principle is:

A Thinking you will achieve success now

B Thinking you will achieve success sometime

C Thinking you will achieve success soon

D All of the above

4. An afformation is:

A Thinking positive thoughts

B Giving reasons why you will be successful

C Hoping for success

D Giving excuses to accept failure

6. Reflection – Positive Vision Board Activity (twelve points: four points per box)

There really are no wrong answers – perhaps just better answers. This is an exercise where you need to really listen at first, and then add your views in a questioning way so that the young person still owns their answer!

OR

6. Create your own Afformation Card

(maximum twelve points)

Write down sayings that are positive with reasons or evidence why you will be successful. Encourage inter-class talk about what sayings they have heard and like, or can they create their own. Be aware of poor examples of sayings that have flawed thinking, e.g. "no pain no gain" is not always correct!

This activity allows you to work on potentially all six levels of Bloom's Taxonomy!

Levels 1 and 2 - Knowledge and comprehension, i.e. facts and memory

Levels 3 and 4 - Application and analysis, i.e. applying theories and challenging

Levels 5 and 6 - Evaluating and creativity, i.e. new ways of thinking and doing

7. Draw a Poster to Represent What You've Learnt in Mission Three (one point for each of ten pieces of evidence - 10 max)

8. Cuppa's Top Tips (twenty points)

- ✓ Don't let yourself down by using **negative** words with others. Those words can be the start of a **downward** spiral where Self-**esteem** is destroyed and **confidence** is never achieved. Always try to be **positive**.

- ✓ **Practise** positive thinking regularly - it can soon turn into an automatic good habit where positive thoughts, words, feelings and actions occur naturally. Dismiss **the chimp** as soon as it enters your mind. Replace it with a **Jessica**.

- ✓ When you think of reasons why you are going to be successful before you perform a task this is called an **afformation**.

- ✓ Tell your parents or friends at least **three** good things you did today. This is called the **Today Result** and helps you become confident.

- ✓ Tell your parents or friends at least **one** good thing you are going to do tomorrow. This is called the **Tomorrow Promise**.

- ✓ Both the Today Result and Tomorrow Promise are great examples of a **good habit**.

- ✓ Take **opportunities** when they arrive. You may just enjoy the chance to show people what you can do!

- ✓ If you can **think** it, you can **achieve** it. This is the **TA Principle**.

✓ When you talk, think and feel positive, you are in **positive self-talk**.

✓ If you get nervous just **Think-Feel-Do**.

Now challenge your parents or adults to see if they have read their book ...

1. What does Pete Positivity always say?

Think positively – it's so easy to do!

2. What does Rick Hansen say about the rest of his life?

The best years of my life are still ahead of me.

3. Complete this sentence: if you can think it, you can ....!

Achieve it.